Foreword

Welcome to our *Book of Silly Book Titles*, which David and I had great fun compiling and deciding which to include or discard. It became a bit obsessive, so we apologise if you find yourself *hooked* into inventing some of your own.

For a fun starter, why not try to find our favourite eight authors as listed below and discover the silly book titles we've imagined them writing?

1. Lucy Lastic
2. Wendy Boughbreaks
3. Mandy Lifeboats
4. Tara Fornow
5. Minnie Bits
6. Chris Peaduck
7. Henrietta Parrot
8. Dan Spartner

Good luck, and we hope you smile a few times as you turn the pages trying to find them !

Ceiling Coverings

By Celine Tiles

Keeping the Mouth Moist

By Alex Wet

Amorous loving

By Pascha Nutt

Old Drink Containers

By Demi John

Simple Children's Games

By Pattie Cake

Baggy Underwear

By Lucy Lastic

THE BOOK OF SILLY BOOK TITLES

A Pun-Packed Collection of Hilariously Titled Books and Their Imaginary Playful Authors

BY: CHRISTOPHER SELWAY & DAVID MEHEW

Copyrights © By Christopher Selway & David Mehew

All Rights Reserved

No part of this book may be reproduced or transmitted in any form by any means, electronic or mechanical, including photocopying and recording, or by any information storage and retrieval system, except as may be expressly permitted in writing from the author.

Benefit of the doubt

By Lee Way

Touch and Go

By Jed Perdy

The Life of a Mid-wife.

By Dee Liver

Be Warned

By Mark Mywords

Turning Up the Volume

By Mike Rophone

Misfiring rifles

By Rick O'Shea

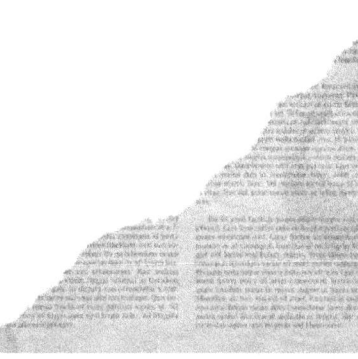

Regimental History

By Millie Terry

The Long Good-Bye

By Tara Fornow

I Won't Keep On

By Andy Stopped

He Denied Everything

By Betty Knew

A History of Great Goals

By Cora Niceone

Managing Your Money

By Bill Topay

Small is Beautiful.

By Minnie Bits

How to Congratulate

By Pat Ontheback

Making Your Mind Up

By Willie Ornott

Robbing Banks

By Barry Clava

My 3 Husbands

By Polly Gamy

Leather Goods

By Tanya Hide

Chocolate Mountains

By Toby Lerone

Singing Other People's Songs

By Carrie Okie

The Chinese Recipe Book

By Chris Peaduck

Looking After Schools

By Jan Itter

Making Small Holes

By Brad Awl

A Gamblers life

By Betty Winns

The Life of a Murderer

By Ida Killedim

A Compendium of Bird Songs

By Dawn Chorus

Life as a Funeral Director

By Paul Bearer

Pub Closures

By Boris Shutt

A History of Jeans.

By Den Im & Lee Vi

The Vile 8th King

By Henrietta Parrot

Visiting a Podiatrist

By Toby Hurting

Medieval History

By Norman Times

Scottish Highlands

By Monica TheGlen

Fitting Roof Rafters

By Joyce Hangers

Keeping the Peace

By Laura Norder

In the Middle of Nowhere

By Wanda Ring

The Art of Smacking

By Tanya Backside

Canned Fish

By Tina Tuna

Best Ways to Shop

By Carrie Bags

Reading the Stars

By Claire Voyant

American States

By Del Aware, Ken Tucky, Col Orado & Den Ver

Wimbledon Footwear

By Dennis Shoos

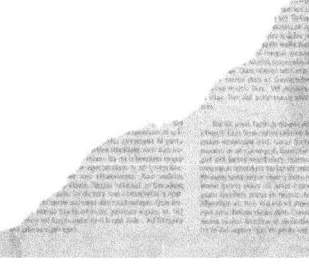

Running Water

By Brook Trickles & Flo Meter

Gone with the Wind

By Frank Le Madere & Ann Otherday

World Languages

By Francis French & Ger Mann

Antagonising People

By Lester Itup

Getting a Good Price

By Cilla Deal

Never Gonna Give You Up

By Cedric Astley

Big mouth

By Lou Slips

Give My Vehicle Back

By Yasmin Macar

My Unhappy Life

By Malcom Tent

The Haunted House

By Xena Ghost

The Estate Agent

By Zelda House

The Boy Scout Movement

By Bob Ajob

Life on the Waves

By Bob Along

Fighting Aliens

By Ray Gunn

Seagulls on My Head

By Cliff Top

Satan in the Forest

By Evelyn Woods

Making Mistakes

By Mable Supp

Me and Him

By Ian Eye

I Barely Made It

By Justin Time

Man in a Suitcase

By Samson Nite

Crossing the Road

By Jay Walker

Flower Gardens

By Rose Bed & Chris Anthemum

The Story of Brown Sugar

By Demi Rara

When the Wind Blows

By Wendy Bough-breaks

Standing Back

By Hugo First

Memoirs of a Carpet Fitter

By Walter Wall

The Business Jungle

By Zebra Meaden

Keeping Secrets

By Celia Lips

A History of the Conservative Party

By Eileen Tudor-Wright

Aches & Pains

By Aggie Nee

A Good Night's Sleep.

By Dee Ream

Life of a Male Feline

By Tom Catt

Nearly Finished

By Albert Over

The Fairly Elusive Barrel Maker

By Maisey Cooper

Desert Heat

By Carl Upandye

Collecting Kitchenware

By Mike Ettle

Demolition Jobs

By Terry Down

Causing Riots

By Cyril Disobedience

A guide to Gambling

By Winnie & Lou Summ

All Over the Place

By Chris Cross & Connie Fusion

The Swimming Teacher

By Davina Pool

The Man with the Boring Voice

By Dulcie Tones

The Trier

By Kenny Dooit

Waiting for Him

By Tilly Getshere

Army Weapons

By Tommy Gunn

A History of Birmingham

By Warwick Castle & Sally Oak

The Nurse

By Hilda Patient

Tales of an Irish Monk

By Ben O'Dictine

DIY

By Andy Mann

Life on the Highways

By Laurie Driver

Life Cycles

By Jenny Ration

I Gave Up

By Peter Out

A Tug of War

By Paul Ling

The Art of Heading a Football

By Eddie Tin

Light Lunches

By Roland Ham

Escapology

By Hugh Deaney

Waltzing for Fun

By Dan Spartner

Sinking Ships

By Mandy Lifeboats

Heavy Showers

By Wayne Dwops

Know Your Boundaries

By Terry Torial.

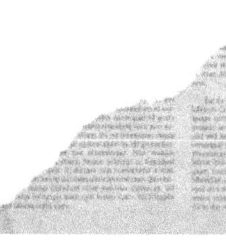

Circus Skills

By Una Cycle

A Life at Sea

By Dec Hands

The Holy Bible

By Chris Tian

The Solarium

By Tanya Bodies

Dealing with Depression

By Fred Up

1960s Seaside Holidays

By Piers Galore

Irish Health

By Steph O'Scope

Jungle Experience

By Ella Phant

The Story of Bed Linen

By Ida Down

Art of Balance

By Jim Nastic

The Chambermaid

By Jerry Pot

Gaelic Cooking

By Iris Stew

The Art of Prayer

By Evan Helpus

I Don't Care

By Ruth Less

Book of Art

By Payne Ting

Driving an Ambulance

By Nina Ninar

Art of Acting

By Oscar Winner

Mediterranean Light Snack

By Olive Forty

Art of Burglary

By Rob Meblind

How to Administer Pee Relief

By Cath Eter

Insulting Language

By Gertrude Comments

Small Cars

By Maurice Minor & Minnie Driver

We Are Closed

By Doris Shutt

The Traitor

By Jude Uss

Takeaway Food

By Donna Kebab

A History of Red Indian Weapons

By Tom O'Hawk

The Winner

By Victor Ree

Firework Displays

By Catherine Wheel & Roman Candle

Life on a Submarine

By Perry Scope

Arcade Games

By Penny Falls

The Furniture Shop

By Abbey Tatt

Death of the High Street

By Will Kinsons & Charity Shoppe

The Art of Caulking

By Cilla Gapp & Phil Itin

Types of Socks

By Terry Towling

The 19th Century

By Victor Ian Times

Conquering the World

By Roman Times

The Coastline

By Sandy Beach

Japanese History

By Sam Urai

Red Fruit

By Tom Atoes

Like Being a Horse

By Don Key

Desert Animals.

By Cam All

Making Suits

By Taylor Ring & Bea Spoke

My Childhood Days

By Todd Ler

The Man Who Stole My Dinner

By Yvette Myfood

Biscuits

By Gary Baldy & Di Gestive

Sport for Ladies

By Annette Ball

Cursed to Die

By Angela Death

Tackling Garden Weeds

By Dan de Lion & Daisy Patch

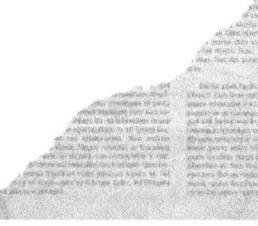

Drafty Homes

By Dora Open

Cooking with Fruit

By Stew Dapple

Spring Rain.

By April Showers

Sewing Old Jeans.

By Fred Bare

Changing Car Tyres

By Jack Itup

I Haven't Got Much

By Matthew Things

Winning a Race with My Wife.
By Pippa Tooit

Hair Shampoos
By Tim O'Tay

Packing Fragile Parcels.
By Polly Styrene

A History of Plastics
By Polly Theen

Amazing Feats
By Stew Penduss

A Year in Parliament
By Polly Tickle

Small Children

By Pip Squeaks

Small Coins

By Arthur Sixpence

Eating Outside

By Alfred Scow

Novelists

By Rita Book

Sitting on the Beach

By Dec Chair

Life as A Couple

By Maria Goodman

Thinking of the Future

By Tom Orrow

Anatomy of a Leg

By Tony Ankle

City Transport

By Rick Shaw

Ambition is Great

By Claude Mywayup

I Can't See Anything

By Edna Bucket

Dealing with Joint Pain

By Arthur Itis

Winning Arguments

By Anna Nutherthing

Recycling Rubbish

By Morag Anbones

Hampshire Towns

By Ann Dover

How to Be a good Inn Keeper

By Bart Ender

Wrapping Up for Cold Weather

By Donna Coat & Mac Intosh

Desert Warfare

By Lee Jon Air

Storm Warnings

By Abigail Cummin & Lorraine Ishere

Fairground Refreshments

By Candy Floss & Poppy Corn

Romantic Poetry

By Violet Sarblue & Rose Sesared

Running a Country

By Dick Tator

Being a Superstar

By Stella P Formance

Chemistry Sets

By Tess Tube & Bernie Bunson

Bristol Suburbs

By Cliff Ton, Noel Park & Lawrence Hill

Weddings Are Fun

By Marian Agin

Tell Me Everything

By Diana Noe

Parlour Games

By Dom Inoes & Cher Ades

Fortune Telling

By Claire Voyant

The Fog is Lifting

By Hazel Clear

www.ingramcontent.com/pod-product-compliance
Lightning Source LLC
Chambersburg PA
CBHW052045070526
44584CB00018B/2623